Nasreddin H

100 comic tales in verse

also by Raj Arumugam:

Nasrudin, the world's best-loved wise fool

cover picture with kind permission of balavenise (flickr); other pictures in public domain

Nasreddin Hodja

100 comic tales in verse

Raj Arumugam

....the stories of Nasreddin represent, at one level, the whole of human behavior...the stories reflect the duality and contrary states in our mind and actions: at one moment Nasreddin is wise, in another story he is the fool; in one story he is kind, in another he can be mean; in one he exists to satisfy his physical appetites - in one he is sublime; in one he is a cheat, in another he is the victim; in one story he is honest and brave - and yet in another he is dishonest and is a sycophant.....what are we to make of such a mix of traits in one person, in the figure of Nasreddin?

It is a reflection, if one is honest, of the multiplicities in one's own mind and being...one simply has to observe one's own mind and thoughts to see this...Often one is quick to find fault in others and yet one does not see the same defect in oneself...

And so in this book, Nasreddin says to those who laugh at him:

Yes, you may see the humor;
but I don't think you see the irony

Nasreddin in class

see
this is when Nasreddin is little
and Nasreddin is in class

his teacher interrupts his lesson
and shouts at Nasreddin:
Hey you - boy
in the front row!
Are you nodding off
into sleep during my lesson?

No, Sir, says Nasreddin
I'm trying very hard
to stay awake!

seven tales of Nasreddin

see, Nasreddin
is sitting in class
and talking and telling stories
and the teacher
is angry and the teacher shouts:
Nasreddin!
Since you do not listen in class
you shall be laughed at in future as a clown
and tales will be told of you
and not just one - but at least seven
each time you are spoken of

Hodja means teacher...and yet, in many of the stories of Nasreddin Hodja, he does not seem to be the Hodja...it is the other characters who appear in one story and disappear completely that seem to be the teacher...it appears Nasreddin cannot teach - it is the nameless others who can teach and so they teach Nasreddin Hodja...and so often we have this reversal of roles of the teacher and the one who learns - the teacher becomes the student and the student becomes the teacher...the difference becomes blurred...one wonders what this blurring means...perhaps it points to the lesson to be learned in inquiry into the self, into truth: one is one's own teacher, for it is one who must see truth oneself...

Nasreddin hard at work

Nasreddin is in his teens
and he works at the warehouse

see, each worker
lifts three sacks a time
and puts them on a pile
and walks back for more

but see Nasreddin
how he works:
he carries just one bag
and puts it on a pile
and walks back for one more

Now, says the foreman
why is it you only carry one sack
when others carry three at a time?

Sir, says Nasreddin
I carry one bag a time
and make three trips in all
But the others
unlike me
are just
too lazy to make three trips

vow of silence

Nasreddin joins the monastery;
he must stay in isolation
and is allowed to say two words
every two years

two years pass
and Nasreddin is brought before
the Elders
and he is allowed his two words
cold room, he says

two years later
again Nasreddin is brought before
the Elders
and he is allowed his two words
bad food, he says

two years later
Nasreddin is brought before
the Elders
and he is allowed his two words
bad music, he says

two years later
again Nasreddin is brought before
the Elders
and he is allowed his two words
I quit, he says

Not surprising, say the Elders
All you have done since you came here is to complain

Nasreddin's gold

see how young
Nasreddin is
and he's on his donkey
in the town square
and his friends ride slowly with him

then in mischief
and with a wink to his friends
Nasreddin shouts to the market crowd:
Gold! Gold! Gold!
They've just discovered gold
in the woods in the South!

and see, everyone disappears
Everyone runs
when they hear of the gold
Everyone runs South
where Nasreddin says they
found gold

and see
the town square is empty
And Nasreddin laughs
And his friends laugh
And suddenly Nasreddin is grim
and he shouts and he rides his donkey
and Nasreddin rides his donkey fast and shouts to go faster
and his friends are bewildered and they ride after him
and they say:
Nasreddin! Where are you going?

and listen! - Nasreddin shouts back
and he screams, still riding furiously:
Gold! Gold! I too am going for the gold!

But, shout his friends – *it's a lie;*
there's no gold
Remember?
You were just playing a trick
on the crowd!

Yes, says Nasreddin, urging his donkey to be even faster
Yes, I know! But look – everyone's gone!
So many people believe in it
it must be true!
So let's go: Gold! Gold! Gold!

Nasreddin's mum offers advice

1

I can't get any girl to talk to me
says Nasreddin to his mother
I don't seem to be able
to impress the girls

Well, says Nasreddin's mum
cool and composed
In these parts of the country
they like their religion
So talk at length to the girls
about religion and theology

2

two months later
Nasreddin's mum asks him
if he has had any success
with girls
Has he heeded her advice…?

Oh, I took your advice all right,
says Nasreddin
And I talked at length about religion
and theology to a beautiful girl –
and she was so impressed
in fact she was so impressed,
she has gone away to become a nun
Now mum, I'm still without a girlfriend…

Nasreddin's donkeys

1
it's graduation day
and the teacher gives awards
to each :
a book to one
a staff to another
silk or precious stones;
and to Nasreddin
the teacher
gives a donkey

2
it is some years
and the teacher
hears of Nasreddin's fame
and comes to visit
the House of Prayer Nasreddin oversees
and to pay homage to the Saint
buried just beside

3
O Nasreddin,
says the teacher -
how great your fame
and vast your following
Tell me, which Eminent Saint
is buried in the mound
beside the House of Prayer
you oversee?

O Master,
says Nasreddin
It's the donkey
you gave me
It died just four years after
and I buried him here
And everyone wants a Saint
so I have not disabused people
of their faith

4
The teacher nods with a smile
and Nasreddin continues:
But tell me Master –
which Eminent Saint is buried in the mound
beside the House of Prayer
you oversee?

Ah, Nasreddin, says the teacher
though people believe it's a Saint
it's really your dead donkey's mother

Nasreddin climbs the tree

Nasreddin's villagers
want to see the world
they want to know what lies beyond
and they want to see what is next
and Nasreddin obliges
and he asks them to gather below a tree

and Nasreddin climbs up the tree
and when he is high above in the tree
he shouts out to the villagers:
I see far and wide
I see beyond and what comes next after our village
and the mountains and valleys
I see lands and I see oceans
I see plains and I see more trees;
the whole wide world is just like our village -
see the village and you have seen the world

And the villagers applaud
and when Nasreddin is come down
they bless him and call him wise
and they promise to remember every word he has uttered
hold on dear to every description he has given this day
and so they go back to their village and their fields
and they go about their lives

and Nasreddin goes to find himself a donkey to ride

Nasreddin comes to dinner

1
see, Nasreddin is plain and simple
and he has no shoes but worn-out sandals
and he is come at the door of his friend
Zali the Ten Times Wealthy
in the City of the Rich
but the guards there will not let Nasreddin in

Get lost, you commoner
You cannot dine in our Master's house
for only the important people and dignitaries dine with
Zali the Ten Times Wealthy

2
see, Nasreddin rushes home
and returns as soon as he can
and this time he wears a leather hat
and fancy shoes
and he has on a silver-lined fur coat
and the guards bow as he enters the gates
and a servant ushers him in to the hall
and Nasreddin is shown a seat beside dignitaries

3

see, dinner starts
and there is much music and fanfare
and there are bowls of soup and gourmet bread
and grapes and turkey meat beside

and see how while everyone eats and drinks
Nasreddin takes off his hat
and he puts his hat into the soup and he says:
Drink, hat! Drink!
And he takes off his coat
and he breaks the bread and stuffs the pockets
with the broken bread and fruit
and he says to the coat:
Eat, coat! Eat!
And he takes off his boots
and he stuffs them with turkey meat
and he says: *Eat, boot! Eat!*

4

And the esteemed guests are disgusted
and Zali the Ten Times Wealthy
is Ten Times Astonished
and Zali says:
What, my dear friend Nasreddin,
are you doing?

5

And Nasreddin says:

When I first came simple and plain
at your gates
I was turned away
When I came again
with a leather hat
and fancy shoes
and in silver-lined fur coat
I was welcomed and brought to sit with dignitaries
and it is therefore apparent to my simple mind
it is the fur coat and fancy shoes and leather hat
that are invited
and therefore
O Zali the Ten Times Wealthy
it is they who must eat and drink

Nasreddin can count to nine

Nasreddins' wife gives birth
just three months after they get married

Excuse me, darling, says Nasreddin
careful not to offend
Doesn't it take nine months
from conception to birth?
Yet you did it in three?

Oh, shouts Nasreddin's wife
You men never understand things!
All right - tell me
How long have I been married to you?

Three months, says Nasreddin

And how long have you been married to me?

Three months, says Nasreddin

And how long have I been pregnant?

Three months, says Nasreddin

And isn't that a total of nine months?
screams Nasreddin's wife
Are you still suspicious?

Oh, I see now, says Nasreddin
Forgive me for asking

Nasreddin sets up shop

Nasreddin sets up shop
in the streets
and his stall signage says:
TWO QUESTIONS ANSWERED
TOTAL CHARGE: $100
PAYMENT FIRST

a man has two questions
and he stops at Nasreddin's stall
and he hands over his money
and he whinges:
Actually isn't $100 a little too expensive
for two questions?

NO, says Nasreddin
What's your second question?

Nasreddin forgets his speech

Nasreddin is an invited guest
to give a speech
at the local assembly of Chiefs

see, now Nasreddin stands before
the crowd, nervous
and he has forgotten his prepared speech;
and the Chiefs look at him
and Nasreddin looks at them
and Nasreddin says:
On my way here
I knew what I was going to say;
but now
only God knows what my speech is

Nasreddin's coat

1
O Nasreddin
it is a cold winter day
and yet you walk about
without your coat to keep you warm
Why don't you wear
your coat, O Nasreddin?

2
Oh no...
I left my coat at home,
dear friends,
to keep my house warm
so it'll be nice and warm
when I'm back home

...the question of identity, that is of the question of Who am I? comes up often in the tales of Nasreddin...is our identity linked to the clothes and the prejudices and the culture we are conditioned into? is our identity our religion and beliefs and our politics and work? what is the self? The Nasreddin tales delve deep into these questions at the most unexpected of moments...

Do you know Nasreddin?

see
Nasreddin walks into a shop
and the owner greets Nasreddin
with smiles and warmth

Have you ever seen me before?
asks Nasreddin

No, no....this is the first time
I've ever seen you...
I don't even know your name...

So how did you know
asks Nasreddin
it was me?

Nasreddin and his turban

Nasreddin in his travels
rests in an inn
and four people share the room
Nasreddin sleeps early
and he sleeps deep and still

one of them in the room
decides to play a trick and he takes
Nasreddin's turban and sleeps with it
on his own head

When they all wake at the break of dawn
Nasreddin looks at the man wearing his turban
and Nasreddin says;
*Oh, that man with my turban on is me
but who am I then?*

Nasreddin dines with the King

Nasreddin dines with the King
and Queen;
and the King says:
So Nasreddin
did you like the chicken soup?

It's the best item
in our dinner tonight, O Great King
says Nasreddin

Oh really? says the King
I thought the chicken soup was the worst dish
The best was the mutton tonight

Oh, of course, says Nasreddin
The chicken soup was the worst dish
The best was the mutton tonight

But just a little earlier you said, Nasreddin
says the Queen smiling
the chicken soup was the best dish tonight

Oh yes, O Great Queen
says Nasreddin
but I serve my King and Queen
and not chicken soup and mutton

Nasreddin sees a face at the window

see
Nasreddin comes to the mansion
to meet his rich friend Mamut
and sees Mamut at the window
having his meal

and now Nasreddin knocks at the door
and Mamut's son opens the door
and he announces:
Oh, Sir - my father will not be able to see you;
he is out on urgent business
and will not be back for hours

Oh? says Nasreddin
All right then. I'll go
but just tell your father, please
that the next time he is out
he should not leave his face at the window

Nasreddin riding his donkey

1
come, come all
O all neighbors and children
Oh come and gather in the streets
or be at your window
or at your door
O see Nasreddin on his donkey

2
O…see Nasreddin!
O…see his donkey!
O – Nasreddin is seated on his donkey!
O – see Nasreddin and his donkey:
donkey faces one way
and Nasreddin is seated
facing the opposite way!

3
Oh Nasreddin, why does Donkey
face one way
and you are
seated facing the other?

4
Oh - Donkey and I cannot agree
which way we want to go
and so neither follows the other

could I borrow your donkey, Nasreddin?

Nasreddin's friend visits him
and asks to borrow
his donkey for a day

Oh no, dear friend, says Nasreddin
moving close to his window
*My brother borrowed my only donkey
just yesterday...*

and just then Nasreddin's donkey
brays aloud in the garden:
Hee-haw! Hee-haw! Hee-haw!

But - says Nasreddin's friend
with a twinkle in his eye -
*I can hear your donkey in the garden!
I can hear your donkey!*

Ah, says Nasreddin, cool and at ease
*Who'd you rather believe?
Me? Or a donkey?*

...Nasreddin is the wise fool well-known and popular from Turkey to as far as China... ....countless stories associated with him have been repeated since at least the 13th century... new ones are created every other day... Nasreddin is the fool, the trickster, ignorant - and yet he is the mystic, the wise, the insightful; he has no no regard for authority and is himself no authority...Nasreddin is one who transcends boundaries...

Nasreddin's followers

1

see
Nasreddin leads his followers
through the streets and alleys
through the markets and the Houses of Prayers;
and see, Nasreddin shakes his head and bum
and all his followers shake their heads and bums;
see, Nasreddin sticks out his tongue and rolls his eyes
and all his followers stick out theirs and roll their eyes
and Nasreddin shouts:
Hee hee ho ho ha!
And all followers shout:
Hee hee ho ho ha!

2

and the Visiting Intellectual asks Nasreddin:
What are you doing
leading these people like donkeys
through the streets?

and Nasreddin replies:
I am leading them, Sir
to Heaven or Enlightenment as they will

3

and how, queries the Intellectual
will you know
they have reached Enlightenment or Heaven
as they will?

Each day, Sir, says Nasreddin
I look to see who are no longer following
and such ones have reached Enlightenment
or have gained Heaven, as one desires…
And now Sir, if you don't mind,
I must go lead a few more hundred
running round the coconut trees
screaming:
Hee hee ho ho ha!

Nasreddin - radical or conventional?

1
Ah, Nasreddin Hodja
tell us truly
if you are conventional
or radical?
Are you truly acceptable?

2
Ah, dear friend -
that depends all
on which bunch of fanatics
rules at the moment

Nasreddin eats the seeds

see
Nasreddin sits eating
dates…
Oh, but do you see?
Nasreddin eats the seeds too…

O Nasreddin, Nasreddin
why do you eat the seeds as
you eat the dates?

Oh, says Nasreddin
because the merchant who sold me the dates
also charged me for the seeds

Nasreddin gets across

see
Nasreddin is standing
on the other side of the river
Let's ask him,
let's ask
how we can get across

Hey, Nasreddin!
Tell us how we can get
to the other side of the river

But – replies Nasreddin –
you are already on the other side of the river!

...well-known and well-loved as he is, Nasreddin is spelled in many ways:
Nasrettin, Nasrudin, Nasr-id-deen, Nasr Eddin, Nasr-eddin,
Nasirud-din, Nasr-ud-Din, Nasr-Eddin, and Nasr-Ed-Dine...

....while the oral tradition of the Nasreddin stories could have begun as early as the 13th century, the oldest manuscript of the Nasreddin tales dates back to 1571...today Nasreddin has been adopted as a wise fool even by the corporate world...

over a year with Nasreddin

Nasreddin has been going out
with this girl
for over a year
and one day
her father confronts him in the teashop

Nasreddin, says the girl's father
You have been going out with my daughter for over a year
Tell me now - are your intentions
honorable or dishonorable?

Oh, Sir, says Nasreddin
Are you saying
I have a choice?

Nasreddin's girlfriend

Nasreddin has been dating this girl
for over three years
but not once has Nasreddin
spoken of marriage

and today Nasreddin speaks to his girlfriend:
Last night I dreamed
I asked you to marry me...
hmmm....I wonder what that means...

It means, says Nasreddin's girlfriend
of over three years
you have better sense asleep than when awake

Nasreddin's father-in-law

Ah, says the father of Nasreddin's girlfriend
I hear you have proposed to my daughter
So you want to be my son-in-law?

Well, Sir, says Nasreddin
that's not the way I meant it
But if I marry your daughter
I don't think I have a choice

would you lend some money to Nasreddin...?

Nasreddin comes to a new town
and he goes to a store
and he asks the owner:
How's business, Sir?

Business is good, replies the store-owner

Oh then, can I borrow ten dollars?
asks Nasreddin

I hardly know you, says the store-owner
I can't lend you any money

Oh, how strange, says Nasreddin
In my town they won't lend me any money
because they say, they know me too well -
and here you won't lend me any
because you don't know me!
It's a strange world we live in

Nasreddin on the meaning of life

Nasreddin rides his donkey
and is stopped in the streets
by a neighbor

O Nasreddin, says the neighbor
I have been wondering long
and you might offer an answer…
tell me: What is the meaning of life?

and Nasreddin's donkey brays
aloud and brave:
Hee-haw! Hee-haw!
Hee-haw! Hee-haw!

and Nasreddin says to the neighbor:
I believe my donkey has answered your question;
and now, if you will excuse me
it's time for me and my donkey to move on…

lend me a 1000 dollars, O Nasreddin

1
Psst! Nasreddin! Pssst!
says the neighbor
at the doorway
Nasreddin looks down from his roof
where he's fixing some tiles
and sees his neighbor in the street

Yes? Nasreddin asks

Come down, Nasreddin;
I have something to say
that cannot be said aloud;
you must stand at the same level
to hear what I have to say

2
and so Nasreddin comes down
the ladder
and asks his neighbor what the matter is;
and the neighbor whispers:
Nasreddin - lend me 1000 dollars;
I need it straight away...

Come up, says Nasreddin
with no hesitation,
and he climbs
back up to the roof
and the neighbor follows

3
Now here is something
whispers Nasreddin
(once they are both seated on the roof)
that I could not say below in the street
but that can be said
when we are at the same height:
No; now you can go

Nasreddin's advice on carrying a coffin

O Nasreddin,
asks a man
tell of us ritual
and proper procedures -
which side should I stand on
when I carry a coffin:
on the right, the left,
in front or at the back?
O Nasreddin,
which side is proper?

Oh, dear friend,
says Nasreddin
it doesn't matter;
just make sure you're not
inside the coffin!

Nasreddin, Donkey, and wild animals

1
Bang! Bang!
Dong-gang! Dong-Dong,
Ting-a-Dong!

Oh, all day
Nasreddin
is making all this din
in his home
beating drums and his pots and pans

Hee-haw! Hee-haw!
Hee-haw – haw!haw!haw!
Hee-haw!

and his Donkey too
all day
master and Donkey
making all this noise

2

O Nasreddin, why
do you make this din and noise -
you and your Donkey
all day long?

3

Oh, says Nasreddin,
Donkey and I are
trying to frighten away
all tigers and wild animals
to keep away from our town

But Nasreddin – there isn't a single tiger
or a wild animal
a thousand miles
round our town!

See! says Nasreddin
Our method works!

Hee-haw! Hee-haw!
Donkey agrees

Nasreddin's donkey eats poetry

Nasreddin looks in the magic mirror
that allows him to peep into the future
and he sees many marvelous poems in cyberspace

so Nasreddin calls his Donkey and he says to Donkey:
See, Donkey – there are so many marvelous poems in cyberspace
They are beautiful poems

but Nasreddin's Donkey says:
Hee-haw! - what's the use? As far as I'm concerned
the only good poem is the one printed on paper

And why is that? asks Nasreddin

Because, at least when I'm desperately hungry, I can eat paper –
but I can't eat cyberspace can I? replies Donkey

Nasreddin's mirror

see
Nasreddin walks
along in the streets
and sees a mirror
left against a building wall

Oh! what a waste, says Nasreddin
a good mirror thrown away
like this...

Nasreddin picks up the mirror
and looks in it
and then he puts it back against the wall:
No wonder
they threw this mirror away...
What a face!
Who'd want to look
at a face like that!

Nasreddin hides in an open grave

it is night...
Nasreddin walks
in the moonlight
He hears horses
Thieves! Murderers!
thinks Nasreddin
and jumps over the wall
and hides in an open, unused grave

the horsemen stop;
they have seen
a man jump into the grave
and they are concerned:
Are you all right, Sir?
Why are you in the grave?

and Nasreddin answers as quickly:
Why am I in the grave?
That depends on your worldview
I am here because of you
and you are here because of me!

the crowd laughs at Nasreddin

see
Nasreddin is in the streets
he rides his donkey;
and see
the people are in the streets
and the men and women point to Nasreddin
and they laugh;
and the children run behind Nasreddin's donkey
and they roll in the sand
and they laugh at Donkey;
and the youth
throw some old cups
at Nasreddin's donkey, and they laugh

and see
Nasreddin sees all this
and he says to them:
Yes, you may see the humor;
but I don't think you see the irony

Nasreddin and the Emir's poems

1
the Emir has it in his head he is a poet
and the Emir invites Nasreddin
to an assembly

and the Emir recites his poem
with much ado,
with much loudness and gestures

everyone applauds the Emir
for his poem
but Nasreddin is quiet
and the Emir turns to Nasreddin, and says:
*So, Nasreddin – what do you think
of my poem?*

Sir, says Nasreddin
*What you recited is not a poem
and neither does it make you a poet*

Guards!
screams the Emir
*Take this man Nasreddin
and throw him in jail!
Three months let him be there!*

2
three months pass
and Nasreddin is released
and is invited again by the Emir
to another of the Emir's recitations
and again the Emir recites his poem
with much ado,
with much loudness and gestures

and again everyone applauds the Emir
for his poem
but Nasreddin says nothing and stands up
and walks towards the guards
and the Emir shouts at Nasreddin:
Nasreddin – where do you think
you are going?

and says Nasreddin:
Sir – I'll save you the trouble;
I'll send myself to jail…

Nasreddin, the liar

outside at the town gates
Nasreddin sees a sign:
ALL LIARS
WILL BE BEHEADED

Nasreddin enters
the town
and declares
to the guards:
I'm a liar!

and the Emir says:
Off with his head!

But – wait a moment,
says Nasreddin
still on his donkey
I declared the Truth
that I am a liar -
and as I spoke the Truth
if you behead me
it is you who are the liars
for your law only demands the heads of liars
so is it off with all your heads
as well as mine?

Nasreddin preaches

1
it's Nasreddin's turn;
he is before the congregation
and he must deliver a sermon,
an interpretation

there is silence and Nasreddin speaks:
Does anyone know
what I am going to say?

NO! comes the unanimous reply

OH! Says Nasreddin
I refuse to speak to such an ignorant group

And Nasreddin jumps on his donkey and he rides away;
and Donkey says: *Hee-haw!*

2
it's Nasreddin's turn again;
he is before the congregation
and he must deliver a sermon,
an interpretation

there is silence and Nasreddin speaks:
Does anyone know
what I am going to say?

YES! comes the unanimous reply

OH! says Nasreddin
Then I don't need to speak to you!

and Nasreddin jumps on his donkey and he rides away
and donkey says: *Hee-haw!*

3
it's Nasreddin's turn yet again;
he is before the congregation
and he must deliver a sermon,
an interpretation

there is silence and Nasreddin speaks:
Does anyone know
what I am going to say?

some say: *YES!*
and some say: *NO!*

OH! says Nasreddin
Those who know
kindly explain
to those who don't know
And those who don't know
quietly listen to those who know!

and Nasreddin jumps on his donkey and he rides away
and Donkey says: *Hee-haw! Hee-haw!*

Nasreddin meets the Emperor

see
Nasreddin is back
after long travel;
he's been to powerful kingdoms
and he has met Emperors and mighty Priests

Oh, see how the crowd adores Nasreddin
see how they are in awe:
Did you really meet the Emperor of Tukmuktan?

see, Nasreddin nods
with his turban full of pomposity

Oh, and what did the Emperor
say to you, O great Nasreddin?
asks the crowd

Oh, answers Nasreddin, *the Emperor of Tutmuktan*
was on his horse
when I met him in the streets
and he said to me:
Hey! – Get out of my way!
A rude fellow the Emperor is, I must say

stand by your word

ask Nasreddin how old he is
and he says he's forty

tell him that's what
he said 10 years ago
and he replies with a smirk:
Hey – I always stand by my words!

reserving a seat

see
Nasreddin is sitting
in the crossroads
We saw him in the morning
and after work, here we see him
again – he's still sitting at the crossroads

Oh why Nasreddin, Oh why
do you sit at the crossroads all day?
You do not move from your spot
You do nothing but sit there all day

Oh, replies Nasreddin
important things happen at crossroads
And when they happen
always a crowd gathers
and I'm reserving a seat for myself
so I get the best spot to see events unfold
so I won't miss anything

course fees, student: Nasreddin

maybe, thinks Nasreddin
I should learn to play the flute

and so he goes to a master
and Nasreddin says:
I'd like to learn to play the flute
What are your course fees like?

Oh, says the Flute Master
stroking his wide mustache:
$100 each
for the first 3 lessons;
and just $20 for each lesson thereafter

*hmm...*says Nasreddin
I'll start with the fourth lesson, please

an obituary for Nasreddin

they had had too much
to drink and eat
and Nasreddin's friends
are become a little maudlin

one says:
If you were dead
and in your coffin
what'd you like to hear
friends and relatives say?

Oh, says one, *I'd like to hear them say*
what a great and generous man I was

and another says:
When I'm dead and in my coffin
I'd like people to say:
What a great teacher he was,
always working hard for the sake of his students

and so each expresses their desire for praise and approbation
but Nasreddin is quiet
and a friend leans an arm on Nasreddin's shoulder
and he says:
So Nasreddin
what'd you like people to say
when you are dead and in your coffin?

Oh me, says Nasreddin
I'd like to hear people say:
Hey – he's moving!

O Nasreddin, who died?

there's a funeral
and Nasreddin stands in the street
and the family carries the coffin by
and a curious onlooker asks Nasreddin:
Who died?

Nasreddin shrugs his shoulders
and he says:
I don't know who died;
but I think it's the one in the coffin...

Theology, Philosophy, and hunger

Nasreddin is listening
and the Great Religious Teacher
is Preaching
It's an endless sermon
with no beginnings
and the Great One speaks of meaning
from the very act of Creation

Growl! goes Nasreddin's tummy

and the Great One speaks of all Acts
and of Great Believers and Martyrs
and all their Devotions and Complete Submission

and Nasreddin's tummy
purrs like a desperate cat: *Meeoow!*

and the Great Teacher's words are endless
and he speaks of Fire and Redemption
and of all those who have made it to Heaven and Hell

but Oh - Nasreddin is so hungry;
how is he ever going to get the Great One
to stop so Nasreddin can eat?
and Nasreddin puts up his hand and he says:
Excuse me, O Great One
did any of the people in all these stories you tell -
did any ever get hungry?
did they ever eat?

Nasreddin, the generous dad

Dad, says Nasreddin's son one day
I dreamed you are generous
and in my dream
you gave me a hundred silver coins

I am a generous dad, says Nasreddin
and so I'll allow you to keep the money
I gave you in your dreams

Nasreddin, hungry

Nasreddin is hungry
but he has not enough money
He can only stand
outside the restaurant
counting his few coins
and he sees
a man dressed in silk
and silver shoes
and embroidered turban
and with a ring in each finger

Wow! Who is this man so wealthy?
asks Nasreddin of a stranger

That is the servant of
the merchant Bashan
comes the answer

and Nasreddin looks up Heavenward
and he says:
Oh God! Look at the servant of a merchant
and look at me, a servant of the Almighty!

letters from Nasreddin

Nasreddin's letter to his City cousin

Dear Cousin
Your cat died

City Cousin's reply

Dear Nasreddin
How crude and uncultured you are
Since I came to the city
a year ago
I have learned to be sophisticated
I always break news in subtle tones
in careful stages
in a series of correspondence
Let me teach you
You could have started by saying:
Your cat is acting strange
Then you could have made it a little more to the point:
Your cat does not eat
Then you could have said:
I have not seen your cat in days
Only then you could say:
Dear Cousin
Your cat is dead

Nasreddin's Letter, six months later

Dear Cousin
Your mother is acting strange

Nasreddin's umbrella

Nasreddin is walking in the streets
He walks with an umbrella
It's raining
and people use their umbrellas

And an old woman shouts to Nasreddin:
Hey, Nasreddin – it's raining hard
Why don't you use your umbrella?

and Nasreddin says:
Oh, my umbrella is of no help;
it has too many holes

and the Old Woman shouts back in the rain:
Then why did you bring this umbrella, Nasreddin?

Oh, says Nasreddin
I didn't think it would rain!

let the burglar help us

it's night

Nasreddin and his wife are in bed

there's a burglar in
Nasreddin's living room

and Nasreddin's wife whispers
to Nasreddin:
Hey, Nasreddin – wake up
I think there's a burglar
in our living room

Shhh! says Nasreddin
We are so poor we have nothing
This is our plan:
let the burglar find something
and then we pounce on him!

the Headman's funeral

Quick, get ready
says Nasreddin's wife
Make haste and let's be punctual
for the Headman's funeral

And why, says Nasreddin, *should*
I make haste and be punctual
at the Headman's funeral?
After all, I don't think
he's even going to bother
attending my funeral!

the Nasreddin Phenomenon

1

Nasreddin hears of the Greek Archimedes
Nasreddin wants his own name to be made famous
for some discovery

2

and so at the tavern
Nasreddin declares his own discovery:
Buttered bread
always falls with the buttered side up

and so the skeptical tavern owner
spreads butter on a slice of bread
and tosses the bread in the air
And the bread falls with the buttered side down

3

Hmmm! says the tavern owner
Nasreddin, you are wrong
See, the bread has fallen with the buttered side down

Oh, says Nasreddin
My dear fellow – you buttered the wrong side!

Nasreddin's two prayers

Nasreddin rushes into
the House of Prayer and
mutters a quick prayer
and gets up just as quick
to rush off

Wait! commands the Chief Priest
in the House of Prayer
Say your prayers again -
slowly and with dignity!

and so Nasreddin follows instructions
and says his prayers slowly and with dignity
and then he asks the Chief Priest if he can go

Yes, says the Chief Priest
And don't you think
the Mighty Lord is pleased
with your prayer slow and dignified
rather than the hurried
and quick one you offered first?

Not really, says Nasreddin

And why is that? asks the Chief Priest

Why? asks Nasreddin
Because my first prayer was for God;
the second was just to please you

Nasreddin the boatman

1
Nasreddin is sometimes a boatman
See, Nasreddin is in his boat
He rows a scholar
across the wide and deep river

Where is you from?
asks Nasreddin

Did you never learn grammar,
you uncultured man?
snorts the scholar

No, says Nasreddin

Ha! snorts the scholar
Half your life is wasted!

2
see now Nasreddin continues rowing the boat;
unobtrusively
though suddenly
Nasreddin says to the scholar:
Can you swims?

No, says the scholar proudly
Why do you ask?

And Nasreddin replies swiftly:
Cos you can sees
there's a storm and we is going to sink
So if you can't swim
your whole life is now wasted!

Nasreddin, the goat and the donkey

1
Nasreddin hates the goat
his wife adores
There's not enough space in our yard
Nasreddin says to his wife
for both the goat and my donkey

Oh, says Nasreddin's wife
we need goat's milk, so just let it be

 2
and see, it is night
and Nasreddin prays hard:
Lord, he says
Let the goat die
so my donkey will have enough living space

3
it is morning, see
and Nasreddin gets up early
and he runs to the yard
but it is the donkey that has died
and Nasreddin throws his hands up in the air
and he speaks to the Lord:
O Lord! Do you mean to say
after all this time
you can't tell the difference
between a goat and a donkey?

Nasreddin helps the burglar

the thief breaks into
 Nasreddin's house
and starts putting things into a sack
and Nasreddin gets out of bed
and helps the thief put things in

What are you doing? asks the thief, surprised

Oh, same thing you're doing, says Nasreddin
We are moving, aren't we? - so I'm helping us pack

Nasreddin's pots

1
Nasreddin borrows a large earthen pot
from his neighbor Salam
Three days later
Nasreddin returns the large pot and a small pot

What's this? says Salam
I only lent you a large pot
but you are returning me a small pot as well

Oh, says Nasreddin
Your large pot gave birth
so I am giving you the baby pot as well

Salam is clever
and he accepts both pots

2
it's a week later and
this time Nasreddin borrows Salam's
largest silver pot

three days later
Nasreddin comes back to Salam
with a very sad face
and he says:
Oh, Salam...I have bad news...
I cannot return your large silver pot
Oh Salam – prepare yourself for this bad news:
I cannot return your pot
because your pot died

Ho! You liar! says Salam
How can a pot die?

Why not? says Nasreddin
If you can believe a pot can give birth
why can a pot not die?

Nasreddin buys clothes

see
Nasreddin walks into a clothes shop
he tries on a green shirt
and he returns it to the owner
and he says:
I don't want this;
give me the same size, brown

And the owner does as he is told
and Nasreddin walks out with the brown shirt
without paying
and the owner runs
after Nasreddin and he shouts:
Excuse me, Sir – you haven't paid
for the brown shirt

But, says Nasreddin, surprised
I gave you a green shirt
exact size, same brand, same price

Ah, says the wise store owner
But you didn't pay for the green shirt!

But, Ah - says Nasreddin
Do you think I should pay for something
I tried on and chose not to buy?

Nasreddin's clothes fall

Thud! Bang!
Nasreddin's wife rushes to the kitchen
and sees poor Nasreddin sprawled on the floor

What was that? says Nasreddin's wife
I heard loud noises from here
What happened?

Oh, says Nasreddin
Just my clothes
They fell on the floor

Do clothes make so much noise
when they fall? asks Nasreddin's wife

Oh, says Nasreddin, *I was in them…*

all of Nasreddin's belongings stolen

1
each day something is missing
from Nasreddin's home;
yesterday was the kitchen cabinet
the day before all the furniture
and two days ago the carpet

2
see
today Nasreddin hides behind a tree
in his garden and he sees his neighbor
stealing Nasreddin's chairs

3
this evening
Nasreddin waits for the neighbor to leave home
and Nasreddin and his wife and children
rush in to the neighbor's house;
and they sit in the hall

and see now the neighbor returns
with Nasreddin's dining table
and is shocked to see
 Nasreddin and his family

4
Nasreddin, asks the neighbor
What are you and your family doing in my house?

Oh, says Nasreddin calm and cool
You have brought all my things here
and so I thought you want us to move in
here to your house
where it's more spacious than mine
And now that I see you've brought my dining table -
maybe you can prepare dinner...

Nasreddin's door

1
see
Nasreddin is walking in the streets
But see - *do you see?*
Nasreddin carries a door tied to his back
Yes, see
Nasreddin is walking in the streets
and he carries a door on his back

Oh Nasreddin, why do you carry a door
tied to your back?

2

And says Nasreddin:
Oh, dear friends
there are so many break-ins
in our town
and as there's only one way to my house
I thought I'll carry my door with me
so no one can break into my house!

end of the world

O Nasreddin
everyone frightens us
with news
of the end of the world
Can you tell us when
the world will end?

Oh sure, says Nasreddin
I know when the world will end

Really? So when will the world end,
O Nasreddin?

Oh, when I die
the world will end;
and so it is for each

Nasreddin, the goats and the end of the world

How the friends tricked Nasreddin

1
Let's trick Nasreddin
Let's tell him it's the end
of the world
tomorrow
and he should kill his two goats
and feed us all
You six stay here
I'll talk to Nasreddin
and ask him to invite us tomorrow night

2
And yes, Nasreddin has agreed
he sees sense it's no use keeping his two goats
seeing the world ends tomorrow
So I'll see you all at Nasreddin's place tomorrow night
We'll have a feast of the goats he shall kill and roast
Come in your best coats and hats
and bring your best chairs
for we shall feast free in the open
in Nasreddin's wide yard

Nasreddin's side of the story

3
and seeing how my friends said
it is the end of the world the next day
I agreed to kill my two goats
and invited them for dinner

and I made a fire
and my friends feasted
and seeing I needed to feed the fire
as it was dying
I threw in all their coats
and their hats and the fancy seats they had brought
into the fire -
seeing it was the end of the world the next day
and seeing it was no use for goats or coats or for hats
or chairs anyway

but I must say my friends were not too pleased
that I had thrown in their chairs and coats and hats
in the fire
even though they knew it was the end of the world the next day
and even though they were quick enough to have me kill my goats

Nasreddin is thirsty

1
Nasreddin is thirsty;
he's at the donkey races
and it's a hot day
and he's very, very thirsty

the drinks stall is at the other end of the field

I need a drink
he tells his friend
and as Nasreddin walks
his friend shouts:
One for me too!

2
Nasreddin returns
and sits beside his friend
who says in surprise:
Hey! I asked for a drink for me too!

Oh, says Nasreddin, always cool
I had a drink and
after that you were not thirsty
so we did not have another drink

the Saint and Nasreddin

a Complete Saint says to Nasreddin:
I'm so complete
I can only think of others

But I, says Nasreddin
am much more complete
for I can so think of others
that it brings me back to myself

Nasreddin steals tomatoes

do you see?
Nasreddin is in his neighbor's garden
stealing tomatoes off the plants
and throwing them into his bag

do you see?
Nasreddin's neighbor is behind a tree
watching everything Nasreddin does;
and now the owner jumps out before Nasreddin
and he says to Nasreddin:
Aha! Caught you red-handed!
Tell me what you are doing in my garden!

Oh, says Nasreddin, *a strong wind blew me in!*

Oh! says the neighbor. *And how do you explain*
how the tomatoes went missing from my plants?

Oh, says Nasreddin, *I didn't want to be blown away*
by the strong wind
so I held on to the tomatoes
and they came off one by one

OH?! screams the angry neighbor
And how do you explain the fact that
the missing tomatoes are in your bag!

Oh, says Nasreddin, as cool as a cucumber
You know what? I was just standing here as you came
wondering about that
Amazing isn't it, how tomatoes can fly of their own accord
and willing
into a bag?

Nasreddin in the cold

Nasreddin is in simple clothes;
and the passer-by is heavily-dressed
to keep himself warm in the cold

How is it, Sir, asks the passer-by
I can still feel cold though
dressed in coat and hat
and you wear so little and yet seem unaffected?
Do you not feel the cold?

Oh, replies Nasreddin
I cannot afford to feel the cold,
while you have wealth enough to feel it

Nasreddin plays the guitar

see
Nasreddin is in the town square
and he has a huge sign by his side:
EXPERT GUITARIST
and see, he plucks on just one string
minute after minute
for an hour

You an expert guitarist?
mocks a passer-by
You sure you can even play the guitar?
I've heard you the past ten minutes
just plucking on one string;
guitarists use all or many strings
and play a variety of tunes
and yet you just pluck on one string
the same boring unbearable drone!

Oh Sir, says Nasreddin
most guitarists play on various strings
to find the perfect string -
but I have found the perfect string so I only play one
And most guitarists play various tunes
to find the perfect tune - but I have found it
and so I only play the one!

Nasreddin brings back the moon

see
Nasreddin comes out at night
to his courtyard
and he goes to his well
to get some water

Oh! what does Nasreddin see
when he looks into the well?
Nasreddin sees the moon
in the water at the bottom of the well

Oh! says Nasreddin
the moon has fallen into the well
and is about to drown!
I must save the moon!

and quickly Nasreddin throws the bucket
down into the well
and he pulls up
the bucket and the moon
Quickly, quickly
Nasrudin pulls
and he pulls so hard to save the moon
so hard Nasrudin pulls, he falls over
and down on the ground he falls
and there in the sky Nasreddin
sees the moon
the moon - lovely, floating and safe in the sky

Ahem! says Nasreddin
smiling to himself and proud
I've saved the moon
and the moon is back in the sky!
Wait till I tell my wife
what great deed I have done this night!

Nasreddin's chair and egg

1
Do you see
Nasreddin sitting in the busy streets
with his chair from his home
and so far from his home?
Do you see him
and he is eating an egg?
Why would he do this
so far from his home?
Come, let us go ask him

2
O Nasreddin
why are you sitting here
on a chair
and eating an egg?

Oh, says Nasreddin
Why? Should I sit on the egg
and eat the chair?

Nasreddin's clothesline

1
come
I hear Nasreddin has
a long and tough clothesline
Come, we shall go and see him
and borrow his clothesline

2
O Nasreddin,
we have come to borrow your clothesline
Please lend us your long and tough clothesline
for two days

3
Oh no, says Nasreddin
I am drying flour on my clothesline

4
O Nasreddin
can anyone dry flour on a clothesline?
I don't think so!

5
Of course you can, says Nasreddin
If you don't want to lend your clothesline
you can be drying anything on it!

Nasreddin's riddle

1
He is my father's son
says the butcher
but he is not my brother
Who is he?

I don't know, says Nasreddin
So who is he?

That's me! says the butcher
triumphantly

2
He is my father's son
says Nasreddin to his friends
in the local inn
but he is not my brother
Who is he?

We don't know, say Nasreddin's friends
So who is he?

That's our local butcher!
says Nasreddin triumphantly

Nasreddin on his fast donkey

1
Oh, see
come and see
Nasreddin is on his donkey
and the donkey seems to be running
as swift as the wind
Oh see
Nasreddin seems to have no control
and his donkey speeds
as fast as a crazy monkey

2
O Nasreddin
why do you ride so fast?

3
Don't ask me!
says Nasreddin
Ask my donkey!

the pathway

The Pompous Religious Leader
(fondly known as PRL)
visits Nasreddin's town

PRL and Nasreddin
take a walk down the road
towards Nasreddin's house

PRL says aloud,
huffing and puffing
so Nasreddin can hear:
Oh, Lord. How steep you have made this path
in order to punish the oft-erring Nasreddin

Oh, says Nasreddin
the path was downhill
and easy
when I came to meet you;
but the Lord seems to have made it steep
and difficult
now that you are with me:
perhaps there's a message there for you

Nasreddin tall tales

like fishermen
mystics too tell tales
and each tells Nasreddin of their magical powers

I can float in air, says one mystic

I can fly to the moon and back, says another

I can stay underwater without air for ten days
says another

And I, says Nasreddin, not to be beaten
I can see even in the darkest of nights!

Oh yeah? says one mystic to Nasreddin
Then how come I've seen you with a torch at nights?

Oh, says Nasreddin, *because unlike me
others can't see in the dark*

Nasreddin and the evolutionist

the evolutionist asks of Nasreddin:
Which is the wiser?
Donkey or man?

The donkey, naturally, says Nasreddin

How is that? asks the evolutionist
surprised at Nasreddin's swift reply

and Nasreddin says:
The donkey never asks for more burden than it can carry;
but man - ah, they ask for more
and take on more than they should

identify yourself, Nasreddin

Nasreddin, riding his donkey
arrives at the city gates

Identify yourself!
shouts the guard
at the gates

Sure, says Nasreddin
and he takes out a mirror
looks in the mirror
and Nasreddin says:
Sure, it's me...

Nasreddin finds five coins

Nasreddin is young
poor and hungry
Nasreddin wanders the streets
in search of a job
but it is past lunch
and Nasreddin is hungry

Almighty God, says Nasreddin
if you would drop me five coins
in my way on the ground
I'll able to have lunch

and indeed round the bend
at the next street end
Nasreddin finds five coins
on the ground

Nasreddin picks up the coins
and he is glad
for this will get him lunch
and he turns first to the Lord up there high in the sky
and Nasreddin says:
Lord - ignore my last request for five coins;
I've found them!

wise people

It's a wonderful world;
it's full of the wise
says Nasreddin

How is that? asks his friend

says Nasreddin:
Well, the other day
I met Mahmoud
and I tell him my wife has given birth
and he asks me if it was a boy
and I say no
and he says immediately,
Oh I see - you have a daughter!
Now, how did he know?
That's why I say
the world is full of the wise

who are you?

Nasreddin is in the tea shop
and a stranger sits beside him
and they start talking
and they talk about family, school, the old days
children, business and work and local news
and the neighbors

now the stranger must go
and he says goodbye to Nasreddin
and Nasreddin says:
By the way, who are you?

the stranger laughs
and he says:
Don't you know?

No, I don't, says Nasreddin

And you've been talking to me the past hour?
asks the stranger, puzzled

Well, I saw you, says Nasreddin
*with your beard and turban
and your white clothes and I think
I have mistaken you for someone else*

Who? asks the stranger

Me, says Nasreddin

Nasreddin's silver coins

see
Nasrudin is in his basement
He accidentally drops five silver coins
and now he must look for them

Nasreddin walks out
to the street
just outside his house
and he looks for the five silver coins

What are you looking for?
asks a neighbor

My five silver coins, says Nasreddin
I was in my basement
and I accidentally dropped the five silver coins
and now I must look for them in the street

Oh you fool!
says the neighbor
You should look
for the coins in your basement!

Oh, how foolish you are! says Nasreddin
It's too dark in the basement
this time of the day
and it's bright out here in the streets
Don't you think I've a better chance finding it
out here in the street where it's bright?
Now, tell me - who's the fool?!

a sack of onions

it is a hot day
Nasreddin rides his donkey
And Nasreddin carries on his shoulders
a sack of onions

O Nasreddin, says the passerby
Why don't you put the sack of onions
on the donkey instead of carrying it
 on your shoulders?

O, you cruel man, says Nasreddin
My donkey already carries my weight
Would it be just to put also the weight of the sack of onions
on the donkey?

Nasreddin's voice in the distance

Nasreddin huffs and runs
and he puffs and runs
through the streets
and the children follow;
and Nasreddin huffs and puffs and runs
and the children follow
and some distance outside the town
Nasreddin stops abruptly
and he starts singing

What are you doing, Nasreddin?
says one of the children

Shhh! says Nasreddin
People tell me my voice is beautiful
when heard from a distance
and now since we are some distance from our town
I want to hear how beautiful my voice is
So be quiet as I sing

Donkey lost, Nasreddin lost

do you see
Nasreddin?
He's lost his donkey
yet he's happy...

O Nasreddin, why are you so happy
even though you've lost your donkey?

I should be happy, says Nasreddin
Just imagine if I were riding the donkey when it was lost -
I'd be lost too!

cow's milk for Nasreddin

One liter of cow's milk, please
says Nasreddin to the milkman
Pour it into this bottle of mine

Oh no, says the milkman
That bottle's too small
for a liter of cow's milk

Oh, says Nasrudin
In that case give me
a liter of goat's milk

Nasreddin's address

see
Nasreddin is in the furniture store
Nasreddin buys a cupboard
at a good price
and there's FREE DELIVERY too...
Nasreddin is very happy

Nasreddin pays and the store-owner
says:
And where would you like this delivered?

My home, says Nasreddin...

And your address, Sir?
asks the store-owner

Are you crazy?
says Nasreddin
Why would I give you my address?
I don't even know you!
For all I know you might send someone
to steal my home furniture!

Nasreddin and the drowning taxman

the taxman is on an official week-long visit
to Nasreddin's Town
collecting taxes and issuing fines

today the taxman swims
in the local river
but is caught in a flash flood
and hangs on to a rock
so he will not drown

Give me your hand!
shouts a townsman, leaning over
from the river-bank

but the taxman does not;
he will not

Take my hand! says Nasreddin
and the taxman takes Nasreddin's hand
and Nasreddin pulls the taxman safe ashore

Nasreddin's magic powers

there is a famine
and drought
and the villagers are starving
The Village Headman calls for Nasreddin
and he says:
Nasreddin...you say you have magical powers
Now, since people are starving
bring forth plenty of fish
through your magic powers
to feed the people

Oh, says Nasreddin
I said I have magic powers
but I never said I'm a fisherman

Nasreddin's tomato morals

Nasreddin sells tomatoes
in his town market

a man from the next town
asks Nasreddin:
How much is a bag of tomatoes?

500 coins, says Nasreddin

500 coins? shouts the man
That's a ridiculous price.
You're greedy - very greedy!
Don't you have morals?

No, says Nasreddin
I don't sell morals
Would you like some onions though?

Nasreddin never pays twice

Nasreddin eats at the restaurant
and walks out without paying

Hey! shouts the restaurant owner
running after Nasreddin
You haven't paid for the food!

But Sir, says Nasreddin
*did you not pay for the ingredients
when you bought them at the grocer's?*

Yes, of course I did, says the restaurant owner

Then, why should I pay? asks Nasreddin
Why pay for the same thing twice?

Nasreddin's Soul

Nasreddin loves his wife
He calls her by various loving names
Darling, he says
Sweetheart, he says
Diamond, he says
Treasure, he says
Precious, he says
But mostly, he calls her: *My Soul*

It is night and Nasreddin dreams
the Angel of Death is here
and the Angel of Death says to Nasreddin:
Hey - I'm here to take your soul

Nasreddin points to his wife who is sleeping just beside
and he says to the Angel of Death:
Well, my soul is just beside me
Did you want me to wake her up?

Higher than the Emperor

The Emperor is out in the country
hunting
and Nasreddin walks into the Imperial tent
and he sits in a Chair of Honor

The Chief of Seats walks in
and he screams at Nasreddin:
Excuse me - who do you think you are?
That seat is only for Guests of Honor...

But I'm bigger than a Guest of Honor
says Nasreddin, cool and still in the seat

Oh, perhaps you are a foreign duke?
asks the Chief of Guards, more subtle

No, says Nasreddin. *I'm even more powerful than that*

Perhaps you are a diplomat
from a powerful nation? asks the Chief of Guards

No, says Nasreddin. *Bigger than that*

My, my, then you must be a relative of the Emperor, perhaps?

No, says Nasreddin
Aim higher.

And the Chief of Guards says with great subtlety:
Oh, perhaps you are our Emperor himself in disguise?

No, no, says Nasreddin. *Even higher than that*

The Chief of Guards loses his cool and he screams:
No one is higher than the Emperor!

That's me - no one, says Nasreddin
with a smile

Nasreddin finds all are right

1
see how well Nasreddin sits as a judge
in the village court
And listen how well and persuasively
the prosecutor presents the case
Nasreddin is so impressed
he says to the prosecutor:
You are right! You are right!

2
And the Defendant's lawyer reminds Nasreddin:
Sir, you should wait for me to present my side of the case

You are right, you are right, says Nasreddin

3
But they can't both be right, says the Clerk of Court

And Nasreddin says: *O you are right too, you are right*

Nasreddin weighs the cat

five pounds of meat Nasreddin brings home
and his wife cooks the meat
and finds the meat so good
she eats them all

Nasreddin returns home after work for dinner
and his wife says:
O I cooked all the meat
and the cat ate all of it

Nasreddin weighs the cat
and he finds the cat to be its usual five pounds
Since the meat I brought home
was five pounds, then dear wife,
where is the cat?
And if this is the cat,
then what happened to the meat?

Nasreddin the fisherman

Nasreddin is in the street
just outside his house
In his hands Nasreddin has a fishing rod
and the hook is in a pot of water on the street floor

The Scholar walks past
and he laughs at Nasreddin:
Hey, you fool - have you
caught any fish today?

Yes, Sir, I have, says Nasreddin
I caught three today
No - actually, I caught four
including you

Nasreddin's fishing net

1
the Town Council is looking
for judges
and the committee goes about the streets looking
for suitable people to fill the vacancies

and see
Nasreddin walks about humbly
with a fishing net on his shoulders

the Town Council committee
sees Nasreddin in the square
and they
laugh at Nasreddin and they say:
You with the fishing net...
Why do you go about
carrying the fishing net?

Oh, says Nasreddin ever modestly
it is to remind me of my humble origins
This is the symbol of my link
with the ordinary people

The Town Council committee is impressed
and offers Nasreddin the job
Now Nasreddin is a judge
in the Town Council Justice Department

2
three months later
the Town Council committee
comes to see Nasreddin but they find
he no longer carries the fishing net
Oh why, says the Committee
do you no longer carry the fishing net with you?

Oh, says Nasreddin quite honestly
you don't need the fishing net
after you've caught the fish, do you?

Nasreddin the fearless

In my time, says Nasreddin
I have made
even fearsome and bloodthirsty robbers run!

Really? ask the friends
at the tea-shop. *How did you do that?*

Easy, says Nasreddin
When I saw them, I ran as fast as I could
and they ran after me

Nasreddin's tomb is not complete

Nasreddin is having his tomb built
Nasreddin supervises the work

He wants this done
and it is done
He wants that done
and that is done
And so on
And after months
the mason comes to see Nasreddin and he wants his money

I can't pay, says Nasreddin
The work is not complete

It is, says the mason
What else has to be done?

Don't we need the body, you think? asks Nasreddin

Nasreddin's recipe

Nasreddin buys some meat
and he walks home with the package
On the way he stops below a tree
and a wild dog runs forward
and rushes away with the meat

And Nasreddin shouts at the dog:
Run! You silly dog!
You won't enjoy it
for though you have the meat
it is I who have the recipe -
and that you shall never get from me!

Nasreddin's dream

Nasreddin dreams
the Sheik is willing to give him
eight gold coins
but Nasreddin insists on ten

Nasrredin awakes
and sees no coins in his hands
and immediately Nasreddin closes his eyes
 and stretches his right hand
and he says:
All right - I will take eight, please

Nasreddin and the birds

the street urchin plays a trick on Nasreddin often;
he has a bird in his closed hands
and he says to Nasreddin:
Tell me, Nasreddin -
is the bird in my hands dead or alive?

if Nasreddin says, *It is alive*
the urchin kills the bird
and laughs in triumph;
if Nasreddin says it is dead
the urchin releases the bird
and laughs in triumph

this time again the urchin says:
Tell me, Nasreddin -
is the bird in my hands dead or alive?

Ah, says Nasreddin
it is all in your hands

Nasreddin does not know his wife's name

So your name is Nasreddin
You've been married 20 years
What is your wife's name?
the census official asks

I don't know, says Nasreddin

How is that? asks the puzzled official
You don't know your wife's name
even after 20 years?

Well, says Nasreddin
I didn't think the marriage would last past five years
and so I never bothered to learn her name
And after the five years
it became unnecessary to know

Nasreddin cannot provide a good meal

A beggar knocks at Nasreddin's door
and says: *THE MIGHTY GOD has directed me*
to this house for a good meal

Nasreddin points to a House of Prayer
across the street
and he says:
Go there. The MIGHTY GOD lives there

...setting things upside down and looking at situations and conventions in a new way brings forth creativity and freshness...and so it is that we see in many of Nasreddin's stories this reversal of situations and roles and arrangements in society and everything is deconstructed for the moment in a Nasreddin story...it's not necessarily an anarchic view of the world but an invitation to look afresh at one's life and values and approach...questions lead to insight and there is no prescription in the answers as the insight and answers are one's own...

...and yet one fails in Nasreddin if one looks for insight and philosophy in each story...the Nasreddin story is an explosion of laughter, of a moment lived....an instance of delight, of joy...it ends there, it is done and it is finished...to extrapolate wisdom and principles is something else...one listens to a Nasreddin story and one laughs, there is a movement in the mind, a seeing, and it is done...

Nasreddin's feet

Nasreddin is tired
and he sits in the marketplace
with his feet stretched out
pointing towards
a House of Prayer
just across the street

You! shouts a holy man
with all his badges and medals
Do not allow your feet to point in the direction
of the House of prayer
for ALMIGHTY GOD lives there!

Ah, wise man, says Nasreddin
show me the direction in which ALMIGHTY GOD
does not live
and I will rest with my feet pointing in that direction...

the rock in Nasreddin's garden

the gathering declares
with great sagacity
how one's strength decreases
with age:
One is stronger when young;
weaker when one is old

I disagree, says Nasreddin
I'm just as strong old
as when I was young

How so? asks the gathering
Explain yourself!

Well, I cannot lift
the rock in my garden -
just the same as when I was young!

Nasreddin on his veranda

see
Nasreddin walks up and down his veranda

you can see NASREDDIN IS AGITATED AND WORRIED
He has been walking up and down for over an hour

Nasreddin's wife can see it too
and she says to Nasreddin:
What is the matter?
what are you worried about?

Oh, says Nasreddin to his wife
I owe our neighbor 100 silver coins
and I said I'll return them by end of the month
which is tomorrow
but I have not a single coin

Oh, says Nasreddin's wife
Be honest and just go and tell him

And Nasreddin takes his wife's advice
and returns within minutes
and his wife asks: *So what happened?*

Oh, I told him all right, says Nasreddin
Now he's walking up and down his veranda

Nasreddin the smuggler

Nasreddin is old
and retired in Owl Town
and so is Matadun
the ex-Borders Inspector

Ah, Nasreddin, says Matadun
seated with Nasreddin in the Owl Town Tea Shop
There's something I must ask of you
something I must know before I die

What is it? Nasreddin asks

All those years, says Matadun
when I was the Officer in charge of our Borders
you crossed back and forth
riding your donkey
and everyday I stopped you and I checked
and I checked your belongings, and did a body search
and I checked all your possessions
and I checked your pannier
and your shoes -
over ten years I checked and yet I found nothing
and yet I knew, we all knew
you were smuggling something each day all those ten years
Tell me Nasreddin -
what did you smuggle?

Nasreddin smiles and he says:
Donkeys...I smuggled donkeys right under your nose...

OK....I lied!

Those of you who actually counted the number of tales in this book will know I lied...There aren't 100 comic tales in verse on Nasreddin - there are 109...

No, I didn't mean the extras to be some sort of a bonus, a selling point as commerce today will have it, but hey - this is a book of Nasreddin tales and that's what you get!

Nasreddin dies

Nasreddin is dying

the whole Town comes to see him
the womenfolk
and the men
gather round the bed
and Nasreddin looks at them
and he smiles and says:
You women all look so beautiful
You men all look so noble
Maybe Death would rather take one of you

Nasreddin smiles
He closes his eyes
Death takes Nasreddin

epitaph on Nasreddin's headstone

keep moving;
motion is good

Made in the USA
Middletown, DE
04 December 2019

79994503R00085